How to Analyze People

*The Complete Guide to Body Language,
Personality Types, Human Psychology
and Speed Reading Anyone*

David Clark

original author of this work can be in any fashion deemed liable for any hardship or damages that may befall them after undertaking information described herein.

Additionally, the information found on the following pages is intended for informational purposes only and should thus be considered, universal. As befitting its nature, the information presented is without assurance regarding its continued validity or interim quality. Trademarks that mentioned are done without written consent and can in no way be considered an endorsement from the trademark holder.

Table of Contents

Introduction

Imagine being able to tell within a few meetings if a date has the potential to be an amazing partner. Imagine being able to tell if the potential customer is indeed impressed with your sales pitch as soon as you finish it. Imagine being able to tell if your potential client or business associate is satisfied enough with the negotiations to go ahead with the deal. Imagine the power to comprehend people's reactions and decisions even before they occur. This is the beauty of being able to analyze people.

A majority of our insecurities are rooted in our failure to understand what others think or feel about us. Does my partner truly cherish my presence in his or her life? Is my boss truly appreciative of my skills? These are the fears and uncertainties that bog us down throughout life.

What if you had the 'magic weapon' or 'superpower' to know exactly what people are thinking or feeling? What if you could read people like a book? It would remove taxing guesswork out of several relationships and allow you to deal with the person more appropriately. When we master the art of reading other people' minds, we can play our cards more smartly or in a way that benefits us.

When you learn to analyze people, you can preempt possible situations and people's reactions to better manage your own responses to create optimally advantageous situations. It equips you with the ability to come to a common ground or consensus with others to accomplish more harmonious relationships and effective negotiations. In a potentially conflict-laden scenario, you will be most likely to come up with cohesive and well-rounded solutions that are acceptable to everyone.

People readers also have the upper hand when it comes to customizing their responses to the requirements of others, thus leading to less unpleasant situations. Analyzing people lays a common ground for you to practice open communication and accomplish greater harmony by understanding the other person/team's perspective.

You will learn to be less judgmental and more objective in your approach to appreciating another individual's perspective.

The biggest advantage of being able to analyze people is that when you read people by observing them or speaking to them, there is a greater ability to tailor your suggestions, insights, and ideas in a manner that is acceptable to others.

You can place yourself in the other person's shoes and can, therefore, understand their weaknesses, insecurities, and fears. Thus, these insights can be used to present your ideas with a conviction that does not anger or hurt them.

Human beings are complex creatures with several personality layers. To understand them accurately, you need to go beyond their words or actions. Sometimes a person may refuse to do something, but an expert people reader will be able to spot the undercurrents or subtext in their verbal or nonverbal communication that conveys that they are still open to the idea and just need a little more convincing.

This explains why individuals with well-cultivated people analyzing skills are brilliant leaders, orators, and negotiators. They know the pulse of their folks and can deliver exactly what people want.

People who practice analyzing others on a regular basis can note the slightest change in the inflection of a person's voice or read gestures or comprehend things left unsaid by reading between the lines. In short, learning to analyze people is the key to personal, professional, and social success.

Brace yourself, grab a cup of coffee, and make the most of this thoroughly enjoyable and insightful book about analyzing people.

Chapter One:

Benefits of Analyzing People

In the introduction, we briefly skimmed through the advantages of analyzing people. Now, let's talk about the benefits of it deeper. What are the rewards of developing this fine art? Well, here are a handful of benefits of being able to analyze people.

People analyzers are wonderful friends and guides

Imagine being able to give pristine advice, suggestions, or guidance to people based on your ability to read them correctly. It gives you the power to solve other people's problems more effectively. Imagine basking in the sunshine of putting your skills to good use for the betterment of humanity. This is your opportunity to be in the limelight if a friend is having a particularly challenging love life or trouble with his or her boss.

Reading people gives us the ability to be more considerate

Reading others gives us the power to develop greater empathy and emotional intelligence. It also helps us become more considerate in our approach to others. We learn to understand other people by gaining a better insight of their feelings, thoughts, perspective, and ideas. There is a greater ability to be able to appreciate arguments that do not agree with ours. This leads to healthier debates, problem solving and negotiations.

We are always well equipped

How many sleepless nights did you spend guessing various reactions of your audience during a presentation? Or how a negotiation will go? Or how a date will unfold? The ability to analyze people takes away the guesswork and puts us in the driver's seat. We are well prepared to tackle any situation that arises based on our ability to read people correctly. Yes, you will always be on target!

Professional Success

Unless you are working under a rock, a major part of your work involves dealing with other people on a daily basis. You are selling, closing deals, impressing clients, handling feedback from your boss, giving instructions to your subordinates, and closely working with your team members every day.

Wouldn't it be more beneficial for you professionally if you developed a natural ability to understand exactly what is in your boss' mind or what drives your subordinates? The sharpest and shrewdest trial attorneys are trained in the art of reading people. This helps them gather invaluable insights about which the jury is tilting. A single twitch of the nose or hand gesture is enough to speak volumes about what the juror is thinking.

Similarly, people in sales undergo extensive training about the art of reading a potential customer's behavior. They know exactly which customer is likely to buy from them and which one isn't, thus investing their time and efforts in the right direction.

Boosted sales figures, more advantageous negotiations, and happy workers and clients spell professional success. This does not come overnight though. It requires consistent practice, training, and discipline. You cannot just wake up one day and be a people analyzer. However, the good news is, you can begin today!

Effective speaker and communicator

Reading people's body language and verbal communication patterns make you an exceptional communicator and speaker. As a presenter, orator, or public speaker, you'll learn to watch out for audience clues to tailor your talk according to their requirements or expectations.

You can make clever adjustments in the way you convey a point to make it more appealing and persuasive for your audience. You will know exactly when to stop or at what point to say something dramatic that instantly grabs their attention.

The speech can be modified to accomplish a common ground with your listeners where you become more relatable and identifiable for them. It becomes simpler to establish a more credible and authoritative presence while reinforcing your position as a leader when you can preempt audience reaction.

Pick better employees and business partners

Imagine the time, effort, and hassle you will save yourself if you can hire the right people for your organization. Can you spot honesty, dedication and integrity in people? Are you able to tell when people are being genuine during jobs interviews and when they are simply fibbing to make a favorable impression on the interviewer? Do job applications really possess the traits needed to fulfill a role/position satisfactorily? As an interviewer or business owner, you have the power to pick the right kind of people to be a part of your organization by reading them.

Think about a situation where you are contemplating to promote an employee but aren't sure if he or she will indeed do justice to the position. Will he or she be able to excel in a position of greater responsibility? Will he or she be able to inspire, lead, and manage a team? Will he or she be able to fulfill specific tasks assigned to them?

How do you pick a team for each project when the organization is handling multiple projects? Understanding people is the key to assigning them to projects that optimize their skills. You will know exactly who belongs to which project based on their strengths and weaknesses.

It allows us to be better partners

Way too many people are stressed about being the perfect partners or lovers without understanding what the other person seeks. If you are having constant disagreements, arguments, or conflicts, you both aren't on the same page.

The ability to analyze your partner gives you control to what you can say or do to enjoy more harmonious and fulfilling interpersonal relationships. It takes the conflict out of everyday situations and allows us to focus on solutions that lead to more rewarding relationships at home.

You'll pretty much know exactly what your partner is thinking and feeling, and will be able to customize your own responses to work out calm and mutually agreeable solutions.

Chapter Two:

Decoding Human Behavior Basics

Countless realms of papers have been devoted to research about human behavior. Of course, it is at the base of driving all commerce, art, inventions, and relationships. It is at the core of comprehending how people act, decide, speak, memorize, and plan.

Why do you think people are investing in sensor technology and multi-modular data collection? Why do you think corporations are in a frenzy to study and analyze consumer behavior and psychology? There is a huge demand for research related to decoding hidden secrets of the human mind.

Human behavior is a highly multi-dimensional and dynamic study field that requires various investigation points to offer accurate insights. You cannot study one aspect of influencing human behavior in isolation to other factors.

Each factor contributes towards determining a majority of our behavior, though it varies according to the environment. Understanding human behavior is a complex task, and learning newer and more evolving trends in the science of human behavior makes it even trickier.

Why do people behave the way they do? What drives them to behave in a certain manner? What influences people's behavior? And how can you use this knowledge for optimum benefit? Here are some of the most important points for decoding basic human behavior.

Classical Conditioning

Classical conditioning is a psychological process through which a human being learns behavior in pairs of stimulus and response. For instance, sour food generally stimulates salivation. The same process is in fact used in pet training too. Each time your pet puppy fetches the ball, it gets a treat. Thus, it comes to associate a stimulus with a response, which means each time it fetches the ball it knows a treat will follow the act.

Throughout our childhood, teen, and adult years, we experience this classical conditioning that molds our behavior. As a baby, we learn crying will get us our food. In our academic years, we learn studying hard gets us good grades. Thus the classic conditioning we receive throughout our life influences our behavior.

Today, it is used as one of the most powerful and widely used principles for understanding people's behavior.

Human Behavior and Physiology

There are certain and very specific physiological reactions to certain stimuli that help us analyze people. Yes, these are the very tools that are used in the arena of criminal investigation.

Using a series of biometric sensors, you can tell whether people are indeed behaving in sync with their thoughts or if they are misleading or manipulating others. These psychophysiological techniques are powerful for deciphering the "whys" that drive human behavior.

There are certain physiological reactions the human body undergoes when people do not speak the truth. It can be anything from dilation of pupils to increase in heart rate to twitching of toes. People do not always display absolute honesty when it comes to voicing how they feel. It may not always be because they are manipulative or crafty. Sometimes, it's more to do with their inability to express their emotions verbally or pressure to give a certain kind of response. It isn't always easy to coherently express your mood or emotions, is it?

Emotions and Human Behavior

Emotion is extremely scientific or clinical. It can be described as a short conscious experience comprising mental activity, and feelings that do not originate from a place of logic or knowledge. For instance, even when we have pressing evidence of the fact that our partner has been unfaithful to us, we refuse to break ties. There is a tendency to act on brief impulses or feelings over reasoning and available knowledge (or evidence).

Thus, people's behaviors are primarily driven by their emotions. The ability to understand people's emotions gives us the power to understand or predict their behavioral patterns.

Subconscious Mind and Human Behavior

There are three distinct layers a human mind is divided into – the conscious mind, the subconscious mind, and the unconscious mind. Consciousness is nothing but a state of awareness of our thoughts, actions, and experiences.

We are aware of everything we are feeling and perceiving. It allows us to process internal feelings, ideas and thoughts that we accumulate from our environment.

However, a huge part of human behavior is driven by unconscious processes. Have you seen an iceberg? It has tons and tons of hidden or invisible layers. Our mind is pretty much the same. It has multiple layers which, even unknown to us, influence our behavior.

Like other biological creatures, we are perpetually reacting to our surroundings beyond our conscious mind.

Human Behavior and Experiences

While some psychologists ascribe a major portion of our behavior to genetics, others are of the opinion that our behavior is merely an aggregation of everything we have experienced since birth. They believe it is experience or the environment alone that shapes our behavior.

For instance, a person who is constantly differentiated against due or race or lack of privileged upbringing may turn out to abhor wealth or class. He or she will be likelier to empathize with the situation of the oppressed or underprivileged. Their life experiences have shaped their outlook and behavior.

Chapter Three:

Body Language Secrets Unlocked

D id you realize how people say much more through what they leave unsaid? What we verbally speak is guided by our conscious mind, which means it is easier to fake. However, our nonverbal signals (body language, expressions, voice tone, etc.) are guided by a more involuntary or automated subconscious mind. This means these subconscious clues cannot be 'touched up' or faked.

When you tune in to these subtle yet significant nonverbal clues, you unlock the secrets to understanding a person's behavior like never before. It is tougher to control what your subconscious is processing, unlike the thoughts and feelings playing in the conscious mind.

While communicating with others, we are sending nonverbal signals back and forth. Everything – from our eyes to facial expressions to postures and voice tone – is adding to the composition of the message, whether we are consciously aware of it or not.

As humans, we have much less influence over nonverbal communication that essentially reflects deeper layers of consciousness. Non-verbal communication or body language is more reflexive, instinctive, and stimuli-driven.

There's no time to think (unless the person is a body language expert too) through your reactions. Unlike conscious-mind-driven behavior, it isn't easy to manipulate behavior guided by the subconscious mind.

If there is an obvious mismatch in the way people say something and do, pay close attention to their body language. These are the hidden clues that help you delve into people's subconscious minds to unlock the true feelings, thoughts, or intentions behind their actions. Involuntary actions are hard to contrive or stage-manage.

Studies reveal that people remember about 10 percent of the information that is passed down to them verbally and approximately 20 percent of visually communicated information. Now here's the best part.

If you combine both orally and visually communicated information, 70 percent of the information is retained. This means body language is huge when it comes to deciphering the true meaning or motives behind a person's actions.

Here are some massively useful tips for reading a person's body language.

1. Set a Baseline

Before you aim to be the ultimate body language ninja, establish a baseline for people's behavior. In a majority of the instances, you will be meeting and forming an impression about people for the first time. There are instances when you get to personally know an individual, which makes reading his or her body language even more effective.

For instance, a person is a speedy thinker, quick action taker, fidgety, and restless. Their mind is forever buzzing with ideas and mental energy. Now, if you do not know this individual well (or you do not know this side of them), you'll read his or her hyperactivity of fidgetiness as a sign of anxiety or nervousness. If you were to randomly spot that person in a supermarket or bus, you'd think he or she was super nervous.

When you have a baseline about people, reading body language and other non-verbal clues becomes more accurate. Tune in to people completely to figure out their baseline or essential behavior. This will help you relate non-verbal clues more effectively. How does someone react to different circumstances and situations? What is their inherent personality? How are their communication skills? How is their speech and choice of words? What about the voice? Are they essentially confident or anxious?

These are all important points to establish before you start deciphering the thoughts and motives behind their body language. When their behavior is suddenly not in sync with the baseline behavior, you know something is wrong.

2. Look for a Group of Clues

A big fallacy while reading or analyzing people through their body language is to look for isolated or individual clues. Look for a group of clues instead of singling out signs. You can make a more logical and accurate conclusion by observing a cluster of nonverbal clues.

For example, you have been told by all body language experts that looking directly into a person's eyes is a sign of high confidence. However, a person's eyes may be hurting, or the sunlight may be too harsh. In the event, you ignore all other signs such as his or her firm handshake, erect posture, and non-fidgety hands to conclude that the person is nervous (simply because he did not maintain eye contact).

Read clues in clusters, which offer a more accurate analysis of what a person is thinking or feeling. Do not make quick and sporadic conclusions based on isolated nonverbal signals.

Again, a person may be moving away from you not because they are disconnected with what you are saying, but simply because the seating may be uncomfortable. Find a minimum of 4-5 nonverbal clues to back your conclusion.

So in this case, what are the person's expressions? How are his or her hands placed? How is he or she sitting? Is he or she maintaining consistent eye contact? All this will reveal if he or she is truly interested in what you are saying.

Similarly, include a variety of nonverbal signals to make the reading even more accurate. Say you can read someone's facial expressions or eyes, along with his or her tone, gestures, and standing/sitting posture. When you include a wider spectrum of clues from diverse nonverbal communication sources, the reading is more effective.

3. Spotting Lies and Deception

This is primarily why a lot of people want to master the art of reading body language. They want to be able to tell if others are telling the truth or acting in a manner that is not in sync with their thoughts.

Generally, nonverbal clues related to lying, deception, and inconsistency in thought and behavior include lack of eye contact or shifting gaze, contracted pupils, hands on the mouth, sweaty palms, increase in talking pace (if the person does not speak so fast regularly), rapid eye movements, physically moving away from people, faster breathing, voice pitch rises, perspiration, stammering, and clearing throat to buy time.

Again, do not make assumptions based on stand-alone clues. Look for signs across different nonverbal components in their entirety.

Sometimes, these are signs of mere nervousness, and you may end up confusing them with deception, especially during job interviews or business meetings. Probe further if you want to make accurate conclusions about the person. Take more time to determine the truth through a series of both spoken and non-verbal clues.

While reading people for deception, it is crucial to keep their baseline behavior and the physical setting and culture/religion into context too. For instance, it may be too cold, and the person may have his arms wrapped around him or her for you to falsely conclude he or she is lying.

Reading or analyzing people through body language is not an overnight process, but it keeps getting accurate with practice. Try deciphering what people are thinking or feeling by practicing people reading skills at the airport, in the train to work, at the doctor's clinic, or cafe. You'll learn to tune in to their actions and behavior accurately over a period of time.

I also like to play an interesting reading people game with myself. Whenever I spot a group of people, I like to guess who the group's influencer is or what they are engaged in discussing. Regularly practicing this gives you an incisive, sharp observation when it comes to analyzing people.

Another brilliant tip if you wish to sharpen your deception spotting skills is to practice it on children. Closely observe a child's reaction when he or she is lying. While adults have picked up the art of deception to boost their personal relationships and social stature, children remain unaffected by this power play. They aren't practiced liars, which makes any sign of deception conspicuous. You can then watch out (even in smaller proportions) for similar signs in adults.

4. General Body Language Signs

One can write volumes about reading people through their body language because it's such a vast and fascinating art. There are some body language clues that you can watch out for while analyzing a person's behavior.

If you are speaking and someone is leaning in your direction, he or she is clearly interested in what you are saying or keenly listening to you. Likewise, crossed arms and legs are a huge sign of switching off or being completely closed to what you are trying to communicate. The person does not really subscribe to your views or isn't confident about what you are saying. Sometimes, people offer wide smiles yet cross their arms while listening to you.

While smiles are more conscious reactions and can be faked, subconscious psychological barriers such as cross legs and arms are hard to overlook. The person is mentally shut off from your message.

If an individual is maintaining a consistent eye contact, he or she may be interested, self-assured, relaxed, and confident. Tapping toes or fingers, on the other hand, can be a huge indicator of nervousness. Shifting gaze or looking in another direction is a sign of being disinterested or disconnected from your message.

5. Smile

You can tell a lot about how a person is feeling simply by paying close attention to the manner in which they are smiling. Do not believe me? You can differentiate between real and fake smiles by observing other clues in the person's expressions.

If a person is truly excited about what you are seeing or happy to meet you, their smile invariably reaches their eyes. You'll observe crinkles or folds at the corner of the individual's eyes if his or her smile is indeed real. Another visible sign is the formation of crow feet and crinkles on the skin. A real smile also lifts a person's cheeks, leading to a bunch of crow's feet under the eyes.

This information can be extremely valuable considering smile is the single largest weapon people use to conceal their real thoughts, emotions, and feelings. It is a widely established conclusion among psychological experts that a smile is tough to fake. There has to be a genuine experience of joy or happiness for creating that specific expression. When you aren't really happy, the expressions will not settle into their place.

6. Consider Cultural Context

What are universal body language clues? Probably something like a smile or maintaining consistent eye contact. It is understood across cultures as nonverbal signs of liking a person or being interested in what he or she is saying.

However, some body language clues are not so universal, and you need to factor them in before making sweeping assumptions about people's thoughts and personalities. For instance, what is regarded as gestures or demonstrations of affection in one part of the world may be loud and over the top behavior in another.

Take Italian culture for example. It is all about being expressive, so there are a lot of loud voices and dramatic hand gestures. However, to someone in the United Kingdom, this may come across as majorly exaggerated or nervous behavior. Excitement or enthusiasm is expressed in a more restrained manner in UK. Thus, an Italian may view regular behavior from someone in the UK as lack of interest.

Understanding things from the cultural perspective make it easier to read people correctly. This is especially true for people engaged in global business or travels, where they are constantly engaged in doing business with people from diverse cultures.

Even gestures can have varied interpretations and subtexts in different cultures. What does the thumbs-up gesture communicate to you? Validation or acknowledgment of doing something well or offering someone best wishes, right? However, in some Middle Eastern and European regions (Greece, Turkey), it isn't considered too polite to go on flashing your thumb at people. Sometimes, simple things (like not being aware of these clues) can lead to plenty of losses for your business or reputation.

Similarly, there are a lot of differences in the way people treat personal space in different cultures. In some cultures, it is all right to be in close proximity with the person whom you just met, while in others (mostly western nations), people use physical barriers (handbags, etc.) to protect their personal space.

I also always suggest to people to look at the setting or circumstances in which the behavior occurs. For instance, the same worker may display distinctly different body language when out with co-workers in a local pub and when in the office premises.

It does not mean he likes his co-workers any less in the office or is less serious and laidback (analyzing him or her in the pub). It just means he or she is maintaining the decorum of their workplace and is more relaxed when out with them.

7. Reading Proxemics

Proxemics is another vital sub-branch of non-verbal communication. It is fundamentally concerned with the amount of physical distance between people (think proximity) and a person's physical space.

Don't we all feel instinctively uncomfortable when people try to invade our personal space by standing or leaning too close?

They may be trying to intimidate you or make their way into your close inner circle, or they may be genuinely interested in listening to you. Sometimes people may try to pressurize you into subconsciously giving in to their demands. As a thumb rule when you are uncertain if an individual is willing to invite you into their personal space, maintain a distance of at least five feet away from them.

They may either appear warm, smiling, and welcoming (which means you are subconsciously being invited into their personal space) or rigid, disconnected and uncomfortable (which means they are not very open to the idea of welcoming you into their personal space).

Chapter Four:

Analyzing People Through Their Words

Assume you are the owner of a fancy restaurant that serves diners multi-course meals. Your servers introduce each course along the way while offering detailed information about the preparations in each course. You discreetly walk up to the assumed leader of the group or the person paying the check and ask him or her, "Hope you enjoyed your meal?" Pat came the reply, "The soup was good."

Now, this simple, seemingly harmless statement can give you plenty of feedback about your food. If you read between the lines, it can mean the rest of the food was average or not worth it. Apart from the soup, everything else was ordinary.

Similarly, aren't we all offended when someone says, "You look good today." We are instantly on guard, "What do you mean today, do I not look good every day?" To this, the person will sheepishly retort, "No. I meant you look exceptionally good today."

We convey a lot through our choice of words, and even what we leave unsaid. Just like eyes are believed to the windows to one's soul, words are a stairway to our mind.

Words are a reflection of our thoughts, and the nearest you can get to understanding a person's inner thoughts, feelings, and emotions are is by tuning in to the words they use while speaking or writing.

Word clues are important determinants of a person's behavior or personality, along with offering an insight into their thoughts and feelings. Of course, they aren't the only determinants of a person's personality but can be one of the aspects offering insights into a person's behavior.

The most effective way to go about it is probably deriving working hypotheses from the words people use, followed by testing it by using supplementary information sourced from other means. You are using additional information for corroborating the hypotheses.

The human brain is exceptionally efficient. While thinking, we fundamentally use nouns and verbs. Similarly, while transforming thoughts into written or spoken form, we resort mainly to using adjectives and adverbs. These words are a solid indication of our personality, feelings, and thoughts.

Take, for instance, the structure of a basic sentence. Say, "I ran." *I* is the subject and *ran* is the verb. Now, any words that are added to a simple sentence structure to build upon the noun or verb can offer solid clues about an individual's personality or behavior.

Here are some of the most commonly used words and terms and how they offer amazing insights into an individual's personality.

1. "I bagged another honor." *Another* here can convey that the speaker or writer already has a series of honors to his or her credit. He or she hasn't stated that already but it is clear through his or her choice of words.

   The person may possess a deep sense of self-importance and may never miss an opportunity to let others know about his or her ingenuity. They may be conscious of their self-image and may need constant validation. These are the kind of people who are most vulnerable to flattery and ego-feeding comments.

2. Pronoun usage can effectively reveal an individual's personality. When you say "I do not really think I subscribe to that" instead of "I do not subscribe to that," it demonstrates self-focus. Even when simple questions like, "How is the weather there?" are posed, self-focused people tend to respond with "I think it's cloudy and rainy."

   If you wouldn't read this book, you'd probably brush off the "I think" as an insignificant add-on. However, it can be loaded with meaning. It reveals inward than outward focus.

People with emotional issues tend to use it more often than emotionally balanced individuals. It is people who struggle with self-esteem issues and <u>consider</u> themselves to be in lower positions who use "I" more often.

3. Similarly, an individual who is not speaking the truth tends to resort to more of "we" usage. There is greater tendency to accept the blame and say "I" or "me." They tend to use more of "we."

These folks tend to eliminate speaking in first person completely. For example, instead of saying, "I haven't hidden your laptop" they will say "This isn't something an honest individual will do."

People with honesty and integrity tend to use words such as *none* or *never more often*. One of the best ways to develop an understanding of people's characters through their words is by pouring over court testimony transcripts. They can be extremely telling!

People who are telling the truth are more likely to use first-person pronouns like "I." They will also use more specific words such as "except." This clearly reveals that they distinguish what they actually did and didn't do. Dishonest people, on the other hand, are not subconsciously equipped to deal with these complicated constructions.

4. Another important aspect that can reveal a lot about a person's beliefs and requirements are his jokes. Of course, you cannot analyze standalone jokes or isolated phrases. Again, like I always say, you'll have to watch out for other clues too. Generally, people's jokes not just reveal their sense of humor but also a great deal about their personalities.

   However, if a child jokingly says to the server, "I want to eat a dish that costs half a million dollars" you cannot but help decode that he or she probably comes from a family that places great importance on money or financial security or he has been deprived on a financially stable environment.

5. Have you noticed how people repeat certain words or words that have similar meanings? For example, "his message was really powerful," "this book has a strong lesson," or "I do not possess the strength to run."

   It may appear like the three statements may not be related. However, there is a very clear pattern when it comes to using the word *powerful*, and it's synonymous.

   Our choice of words isn't sporadic. It is driven or channelized by our basic needs, problems, and concerns. The person who uses these words is more focused on strength or power.

He or she may be a person who yearns to be strong or powerful but is bogged down by feelings of weakness or inadequacy. They may want to gain more power or become stronger. Again, very revealing!

6. People can also be read and analyzed by their social media posts. A majority of what people like, write, and share on the social media is a direct reflection of their personality and beliefs. You can gather a whole of social footprint or data to analyze people over a period of time.

    However, you need a large number of posts to come to a near accurate conclusion about a person's behavior or personality. Picking up random, few and far between posts may not be very effective because people's moods can frequently change. Sometimes we write or share posts under the influence of temporary emotions.

    Also, you need to link various posts for finding a common, underlying thread between all posts. A majority of the times, you'll find a clear theme highlighted in all posts that point to a specific behavior pattern.

    For instance, people who lack self-esteem, yearn to be accepted, and desperately want to fit in may not shy away from showing off or underplaying their acquisitions and accomplishments.

A majority of an individual's social media posts point to a single direction, which makes it easier to decode their personality. Even the pictures, memes and videos a person share is important from the perspective of understanding his or her personality through the social media. Would you *really* share something that is against your inherent personality or beliefs?

People share things that are congruent with their beliefs because they seek validation for what they believe in. The need to be accepted and to seek approval from others is socially wired in humans. People post specific posts on the social media to gain support or validation from their social circle.

Is there a particular word that is being frequently used in an individual's post? We've seen how certain words people used can convey their hidden desires, core beliefs, and subconscious psychological motives.

For instance, if someone is constantly using words such as, "achieve," "wealth," "success," "strive," "dreams," "objectives," the person may be ambitious or goal oriented. It reveals your inner psychological objectives.

Similarly, if the individual is joking about money or the amount of money a famous personality makes or a brand new expensive car, you can identify a clear desire to make lots of money. They may make jokes about rich people or people's spending habits. There will be a clear and easily identifiable pattern.

Do the person's words match their pictures? For instance, if the person is using words such as "self-reliant," "rule my own life," "independent," etc. and have a lot of selfies or solo pictures on their page, you can conclude they are almost always self-reliant.

7. You can also establish someone's baseline by asking questions like, "How are you doing today?" You are actually setting a platform for asking more questions. The clues hidden in their answers can establish a clear baseline.

This method is generally used by salespersons for establishing the baseline of their potential customers. They will start by asking their potential buyers how they've been doing or how their day went, and will open the conversation up for more detailed probing and discussion.

The trick to establishing a person's baseline through words is by asking open-ended questions. They will give you insights into how the person is thinking and feeling. Use the above tips to read their words carefully before coming to a conclusion.

8. Okay, so we aren't all trained FBI personnel who can analyze potential criminals through their verbal and non-verbal clues. However, there are still plenty of ways in which you can decode a person's thoughts and behavior.

An important part of analyzing people through their verbal communication is to pay close attention to the words they emphasize while talking. For instance, if your manager says, "I am firm about my decision to scrap this project." His emphasis is on firm, which means there is no way he is going to change his decision.

His choice of words and emphasis indicates that he's pretty damn sure not giving in to anything. The words we use and emphasize on are clear indicators of our thoughts, emotions, and feelings.

Our choice of words is filled with meaning. We do not use words very consciously. They are guided more by the thoughts and feelings held in our subconscious mind. Words people use conveys a lot about their personality.

If someone is constantly emphasizing on the word "hard-work," they may most likely be more driven by challenges or their goals. They may be concerned with fulfilling long-term goals than short-term pleasures. It may be an indicator of a person who is reliable, resolute and dependable when it comes to completing given tasks.

Similarly, the manner in which we elevate or lower out pitch can be a reliable indicator

Chapter Five:

Psychological Theories Influencing People's Personalities

Psychology is a scientific discipline concerned with the study of human behavior and mental/emotional processes with the purpose of uncovering why we think or behave the way we do.

Multiple theories are ruling how various psychologists have approached and studied human behavior. Each of these theories offers a handy framework for analyzing human behavior.

Here are some of the most common and significant psychological theories for analyzing people.

Biological

This theory emphasizes the role of biological influences in shaping our personality. It essentially states the culmination of the results of genetics, nature, and evolution.

The basic premise is that any behavior and mental patterns can be identified using human physiology. Biopsychologists are mainly concerned with understanding human through the study of the brain and our central nervous system.

Biopsychologists analyze how genetics, nervous system, and a bunch of hormones affect your personality or behavior. They explore the link between our primary nerves (in the brain) and hormones with mental states.

In short, it simply implies that we are an aggregation of our physical parts. Every choice we make is based on catering to the physical body's requirements. When someone takes away our food, we behave angrily and irritably.

The biopsychological approach has been used to investigate multiple body-mind linked issues such as linking ailments like schizophrenia to an individual's genetics.

Behaviorism

Behaviorism focuses on the importance of prior learning experiences for influencing our behavior. Typically, behavioral psychologists subscribe to the view that mental processes are challenging to measure without subjectivity. The fundamental assumption is that all our behavior is shaped by our environment.

Behaviorism simply states that our behavior is a sum total of our immediate environment. What we are exposed to within our environment is what we end up becoming. It almost excludes any biological or physiological influences on our behavior.

Psychologists subscribing to the behavioral School of Thought are of the opinion that our mind is akin to a blank slate when we are born. Subsequently, our behavior is shaped by classical and operant conditioning within our environment.

Socio-Cultural

As the name suggests, this theory specifically focuses on the influence of society and culture in shaping an individual's behavior.

While the theory is complex and comprises several parts, the underlying view is that a person's development is learned or acquired through his or her social influences. Similarly, language or cultural symbols contribute to shaping an individual's overall personality.

Animals have a more instinctive, rudimentary form of communication that comprises basic signals. However, humans possess more evolved linguistic abilities that allow them to understand and develop art, ideas, and logical thinking.

Therefore, socio-cultural psychologists believe that an individual's developmental progress cannot be studied by eliminating influences from his social and cultural environment.

They are of the opinion that our upbringing happens in an essentially social context, which means we are a product of our social and cultural influences while growing up. For example, if a child is born in an essentially creative culture, where out of the box ideas and innovation is encouraged, it reflects in his or her thinking pattern and cognitive abilities.

Thus a person who has been exposed to a violent culture or grown up in an essentially violent society may turn out to be a highly violent or socially dangerous adult.

Psychoanalytic

Sigmund Freud is believed to be the father of the Psychoanalytic Theory of Personality. According to him, human behavior is a direct consequence of the interaction between different mental components – id, ego, and superego.

It is essentially the interaction and conflicts between these parts that influence our behavior, feelings, and personality. The conflicts occur on a more subconscious level, which means we are often unaware of forces that are shaping our behavior. Freud was of the view that our personality is a direct consequence of a chain of psychosexual stages.

Each stage represents a constant tussle between our biological desires and societal expectations. These inner conflicts shape our development and personality.

Freud's ideas are not without their share of criticism, majorly because of the singular emphasis on sexual desires as the primary driving factor behind human behavior.

Humanism

Unlike other psychological theories determining a person's personality or behavior, humanistic psychology is not just looking at someone else's personality from an observer's point but also from the individual's eyes.

The fundamental belief of humanism is that every human being is unique and special and that he or she has the ability to transform his or her life at any time completely. This perspective points to the idea that our happiness and our life is in our own hands, and that we are responsible for the life we create for ourselves.

We have an intrinsic ability for self-actualization, which is nothing but the ability to accomplish or reach the highest potential.

Owing to this emphasis on our personal experiences or subjective perception, humanists squash other scientific theories of human behavior. In their opinion, behavior cannot be analyzed using scientific methods because it is mainly about subjective perceptions.

As opposed to the humanistic, behavioral school of thought, the humanist view focuses solely on fulfilling your potential as an individual. It states that all our choices originate from attempting to boost our potential and the quality of our life.

In a broader sense, people are motivated to be the best version of themselves. All their decisions in life originate from the point of wanting to lead a better life.

Cognitive

Cognitive psychology focuses on how the information processed in our cognitive faculties impacts our personality and behavior. It emphasizes that particular functions of the human mind including problem-solving, logical reasoning, motor skills and memory guide, our personality, and behavior.

Cognitive psychologists are of the opinion that our expectations directly influence our behavior. Everything from our logical reasoning to our problem-solving skills in based on our preexisting knowledge. Thus we process past experiences while determining how to behave in a particular situation.

According to cognitive psychologists, how we act or react to situations is largely determined by internal cognitive processes. For instance, you know that there is an important, high-profile office party, where the movers and shakers of your industry are likely to be present.

This information is based on past experiences and processing information around you. Being in possession of this knowledge about the party drives you to behave, act, dress and speak in a particular manner at the party. You have logically processed all the available information about the party that has influenced your behavior. It is our expectations based on past experiences that drive us to behave in a specific way.

Chapter Six:

Impact of Childhood Experiences on Our Personality

Million dollar question – Can our early childhood experiences shape our future personality? The answer is yes.

Now, do not start blaming your parents for all the ills you face in your adult life. What is meant by childhood experiences is your interaction with people in the immediate environment combined with your unique, individual personalities and reactions to external circumstances.

All this gives a clear context to our behavior and personality as adults. The values, beliefs, and behavior we grow up with have a deep impact on our future behavior and relationships.

Let us take an example to understand this better. John was the oldest child and the only male among four children born to his parents. His parents came from tumultuous families and were eager not to bring the same environment into their family.

When, as a young adult, John's mother discovered she was pregnant with him, she decided to get married to his father to escape the filth and move into a calmer environment.

Joshua was a naturally loving and empathetic child. He keenly understood his parents' need and began reaching out to them or lending them support. Joshua believed he could make them happy and introduce more stability into their lives to make them feel secure.

As years passed, he became more concerned, anxious and alert about his parents' condition. He had the same approach towards his siblings, peers, and friends. He felt directly responsible for everyone else's happiness and well-being. He hoped to get love and affection and thought the best way to get love from someone was to make them feel loved.

He started becoming tired, exhausted and worn out because he was constantly giving and getting back very little. He found himself caught in a web of giving and feeling responsible for everyone else's happiness, without anyone lending a thought to his desires.

Now, if you talk to any counselor or therapist, you'll realize these are the kind of children who are most likely to be in co-dependent or abusive relationships, where their feelings are mostly uncared for or subjected to physical/emotional mistreatment. Thus, a series of events in Joshua's early childhood shaped his personality and adult life experiences.

It isn't particularly tough to analyze people' personality and behavior patterns by delving a little bit into their childhood. For example, if someone tells you that their parents really didn't allow them to make any decisions as a child, the person has most likely grown-up to be a codependent adult who has a tough time making choices in life. The child had little control over choosing his playmates or birthday cake or food, which means as adults they are likely to get into relationships where their partner wields absolute control over their choices.

This is how deeply ingrained our childhood experiences are in the subconscious mind. Without even realizing it, people tend to follow the same pattern throughout their adult life.

Similarly, when someone says he or she was born in an environment where their parents reacted to everything in a calm and stress-free manner, they are most likely to experience less emotional stress and frustration during adult life.

As a child, we tend to "catch" the feelings of adults immediately around us, much like a flu or cold. When people grow up in the midst of bright, happy and well-adjusted adults, it influences them too. Likewise, the gloominess is also contagious.

A home filled with exhausted, stressed and frustrated parents puts the kid in an emotionally negative state of mind.

There are theories about how rewards and punishment shape our behavior in childhood. Then there are theories that totally debunk these reward and punishment theories stating that a child's personality or behavior does not cause the intended behavior. Instead, they only learn to become sneakier and do things more discreetly to avoid getting caught (*Drive* by Daniel Pink).

Let us discuss the different ways in which our childhood experiences shape our personality, and how you can read people based on their childhood experiences.

The Early Bonds

Aren't babies extremely vulnerable and completely reliant on adults for fulfilling their basic needs? All our behavior as babies is fashioned for attracting the attention of caregivers.

In the next few months, from mere attention, babies develop attachment. Research has pointed out that this attachment developed with caregivers leads to security or insecurity in attachment patterns in later years. Consistency in attachment leads to a more secure pattern of attachment, while inconsistency in attachment can cause an insecure pattern.

Now, children exposed to secure and not so secure attachment patterns can display varied behavior patterns. Secure attachment patterns are often associated with better childhood performances in areas (such as social skills and problem-solving) and well-adjusted children.

Early childhood behavior theorists explain that right from our initial attachments patterns, we set into motion an internal functional pattern of social relationships. This is exactly why the earliest bonds we form can impact our approach to relationships with everyone from partners to peers to co-workers to our children.

First Friends

As infants, we start displaying an interest in playing with other infants. We learn to participate in group activities and parallel play in preschool. Similarly, we learn qualities (such as aggression in getting what we desire) from others.

How young children relate to their peers or get along with them shapes their social and cognitive behavioral patterns to a large extent. There has been extensive research in the arena of early peer group experiences shaping a person's overall behavior.

Children who are more popular tend to take into consideration the needs of the group when in everything they do. Similarly, children who feel left out are less likely to lead or take initiatives in group activities.

Childhood friendships inculcate important social skills in us. For example, if someone says they've had stable, affectionate, and close friendships in their childhood, there is a high chance he or she is a person with high self-esteem and enjoys more harmonious relationships as an adult.

The reverse is also unfortunately true. Lack of childhood friends is often closely connected with negative consequences, including poor academic performances, employment issues, and reduced mental well-being.

There can be other factors influencing this too apart from early childhood experiences (probably your socioeconomic status or parents' educational background).

Teenage Years

Do not we all start forming our own groups of friends or cliques by the time we reach middle school? In their teen years, people most likely increase interactions with members of the opposite sex to form romantic alliances.

As adolescents, people often pick partners based on highly superficial characteristics such as popularity or social status. When they get slightly older, there is a tendency to pick partners based on values, beliefs or personality.

People's social roles strengthen during their adolescence with clear demarcations such as teens that are popular or rejected. Some patterns that were experienced during their adolescent years (bullying, being a victim) could well make its way into their adulthood.

Someone who talks about being constantly bullied through his adolescent and teen years is likely to feel victimized throughout his or her life unless they take drastic measures to get out of the victim syndrome. However, when you read people, make sure you do not make sweeping conclusions based on their childhood experiences. You will still require more well-rounded data to come to a near accurate conclusion about their personality.

For example, a person may be victimized during their adulthood, but they may also have a couple of close friends who can buffer them from the negative effects of being neglected or rejected by others, thus helping them develop a more positive personality.

Chapter Seven:

Determining Personality Types

The discipline of personality determination is fairly large, complex, and evolving. There are several psychological schools of thought and theories about determining or reading a person's personality or behavioral characteristics. While some psychologists believe our personality is the direct result of the social environment we're raised in, others attribute it to genetics.

What exactly do we mean when we refer to the broad term personality? Personality refers to an individual's unique characteristics closely connected with feelings, thoughts, and actions. It focuses mainly on a specific area, i.e., identifying differences between people and collecting all individual characteristics to understand each person as an individual entity.

Here are some of the most widely used personality types that will help you gain a better understanding or provide a solid baseline for using other verbal and nonverbal people analyzing techniques.

Type A and B Personalities

The Type A and B personality classification were spearheaded by Ray Rosenman and Meyer Friedman in the 1950s.

Type A people are believed to be highly competitive, aggressive, hot-tempered, impatient, impulsive, proactive, in a rush, and multi-tasker. They reveal a greater sense of ambition, laboriousness, and status-conscious approach. Type A personality people are extremely focused on accomplishments and positions, which becomes the cause of high stress.

In complete contrast Type B personality folks are more calm, even-tempered, contemplative, noncompetitive, unaffected and believe in living for the moment. There are greater steadiness and creativity in their demeanor.

They are social beings, and display an easy going, mild, down to earth and low-stress disposition. Type B personality people prefer leading a stress-free and slow-paced life that isn't caught up in a frenzy to achieve things or a high social status. There is a tendency to not rush tasks or procrastinate.

Like all psychological and personality based theories, this one too is dynamic. It keeps evolving according to latest research findings and insights. More advanced research in the arena of analyzing personality types revealed that it is limiting to classify people into Type A or Type B personality because several people are a combination of both Type A and Type B traits.

For instance, a person may be ambitious (Type A), and social or creative (Type B). Thus, some psychologists found it outdated to segregate complex creatures like humans into two personality types.

Type C and Type D Personality

Type C people possess an eye for meticulous details and are completely focused. By nature, they are curious and inquisitive. They are always trying to find different and out of the box ways of doing things. One trait that sets them apart from other personality types is that they tend to place others before theirs.

They aren't assertive enough about their wants or feelings. Generally, they aren't outspoken or straightforward. Type C people are more diplomatic in their approach.

Owing to their tendency to keep their feelings and emotions pent up, they are more prone to stress, anxiety, and depression. Type C personality possesses an inherent need for taking things too seriously, which makes them excellent analyzers and workers.

Type D personality folks display an inherently pessimistic approach to life. Even a small unpleasant occurrence is enough to spoil the next few days for them. These people are more socially anxious and withdrawn.

They possess a deep insecurity for rejection, which is evident in their lack of social interaction. Again, Type D people face a greater risk of being affected by mental ailments. Their frequent bouts of pessimism, depression, and melancholy cause them plenty of distress.

Type D people are less prone to share their inner feelings with others, which is, again, deeply rooted in the feeling of being rejected.

Carl Jung's Personality Classification

Carl Jung personality classification was primarily based on how social they were. He distinguished between two types of personalities – introverts (reflective, reticent, non-social, inwardly focused, contemplative and enjoy their own company) and extroverts (gregarious, social, outwardly focused, outgoing, brave, friendly and talkative).

While introverts were said to be more worried about their future, extroverts were seen as people who lived in the moment. Extroverts were seen as more positive and upbeat about life in general.

Again, modern psychologists found this classification limiting. There was a firm belief that most people display a combination of introvert and extrovert tendencies and are, therefore, ambiverts.

A majority of folks do not demonstrate extreme characteristics of either introverts or extroverts, and hence this classification was built upon in later years to make it less restrictive and rigid.

Myers Briggs Type Indicator

Myers-Briggs Type personality indicator is a more comprehensive and detailed report of an individual's personality. It is based on analyzing people's personalities depending on the way they perceive the world around them and make decisions.

The Myers-Briggs personality test was pioneered by Katherine Cook Briggs and her daughter Isabel Briggs Myers. It borrows from the fundamentals of personality classification laid down by Carl Jung that people are essentially divided into how they experience the world around them in terms of thinking, feeling, sensing, and being intuitive.

The theory is essentially based on the principle that in each person, there is a clear dominance of one of the four functions. We each vary in the way we experience our outer world, which defines our personality type. There is a marked preference for a single function over others, which in turn reveals our inner beliefs, passions, motives, and value system.

Myers Briggs is one of the most popular personality determining tests because it comprises 16 different personality types, making it comprehensive and near accurate.

Respondents answer a bunch of questions that reveal how suitable that are for different professions and interpersonal relationships with other personality types. We'll look at the personalities in greater detail in the subsequent chapter.

Chapter Eight:

Introvert Personality Types

The Myers-Briggs Type Indicator systemically classifies people into 16 distinct personality types building on Carl Jung's psychological personality type theory. Every one of us displays a preference for interacting or responding to the world in one way over others. These characteristics comprise our personality as a whole.

Introverts generally opt for spending more time with themselves, trying to contemplate upon their thoughts before making up their mind. It isn't uncommon for them to latch on to ideas or concepts rather than real things.

Here are the 8 introvert personality types based on the Myers Briggs Type Indicator.

ISTJ – Introverted, Sensing, Thinking, Judging

ISTJs are calm, quiet, reticent and serious, mainly concerned with living a serene and secure life. They are believed to be highly dependable, reliable, precise and responsible. They have a way with logic and are known to possess a rational and practical outlook towards life, with a steady approach towards accomplishing their goals.

There is a deep respect for authority, establishments, and conventional ways of life. ISTJ Type are highly focused on maintaining order, in their physical space as well as life.

If you are looking for an employee/administrator for your business, these may be the most suitable folks.

ISFJ – Introverted, Sensing, Feeling, Judging

ISFJs are quieter, more conscientious, and compassionate. They are extremely focused on meeting their responsibilities and fulfilling all obligations. This personality type reveals a marked tendency to be steady and practical. However, they will almost always place the feelings and requirements of others before their own.

They display a deep sense of respect for established traditions and leading a secure life. Again, these people are highly intuitive about the emotions of others. There is a keen sense of service. Type ISFJ fit very well in vocations and roles where they are required to be of service to others.

INTJ – Introverted, Intuitive, Thinking, Judging

INTJs are creative, original, deeply analytical, independent and resolute. They are the executioners, who can turn ideas into concrete plans. They are perceptive enough to identify patterns in events and give a rational reasoning for the occurrence of these patterns.

INTJs display a high sense of commitment and seldom give up something mid-way. Their expectations from themselves, as well as others, is rather high. INTJs possess excellent leadership abilities, and also make for devoted followers. These are the kind of people you are looking at to gradually take on leadership roles.

ISTP – Introverted, Sensing, Thinking and Perceiving

ISTPs are the curious cats who are always keen on knowing how things work. They display a reticent, calm, and quiet disposition. These folks also possess developed mechanical skills and an interest in extreme adventure. ISTPs are inherently flexible, accommodating, and tolerant. They are observers and analyzers who go to the bottom of a situation for coming up with a workable solution.

ISTP personality types are focused on arranging facts to establish a clear cause and effect equation. They are problem solvers or solution providers who tend to come across as more analytical and detached.

ISFP – Introverted, Sensing, Feeling, Perceiving

ISFP people are reserved, contemplative, sensitive and compassionate. They abhor confrontation or conflict of any kind and are always focused on harmonious resolutions. ISFP will avoid any situation where there is a potential for conflict. One marked characteristic is their refined taste in aesthetics.

There is a tendency to be more broad-minded and accommodating. They aren't rigid about their views, and almost always appreciate views of other people. Type ISFP are innovative and original. They fiercely guard their private space and work within a specific frame of time. There is a greater tendency to live in the moment.

INFP – Introverted, Intuitive, Feeling and Perceiving

INFP personality type people are idealistic, calm and reflective. They are fastidiously loyal to their value system and people they care for. Their sense of beliefs and values tends to be very developed. They are mainly guided by their values and inherent beliefs. They are the folks who are faithful, adaptable, dependable and relaxed. They display a keen interest in empathizing with others and reaching out to make their lives easier.

INTP – Introvert, Intuitive, Thinking, Perceiving

INTP's are creative, analytical, and independent. They are enthusiastic about concepts and theories and possess a deep sense of reverence for knowledge as well as skills. Their demeanor can be characterized as withdrawn and quiet.

They INTPs are generally fiercely individualistic and show little keenness in following the path set by others. INTPs believe in building their own paths.

Not everyone is going to experience an aha-moment here when it comes to reading people. You may identify with traits belonging to various groups of introverts.

Also, bear in mind, when reading people's personalities or analyzing them, no group is good or bad, right or wrong, or negative or positive. It is simply about being different and unique from one another.

Each of these groups displays their own set of strengths and weaknesses, which differentiate them from other groups. It does not make any one group superior or better than the other but just different.

Chapter Nine:

Extrovert Personality Types

A majority of people do not act either in one manner or another in every situation. Our behavior tends to adapt or vary according to people around us and external circumstances. This essentially adaptive quality allows us to vary our behavior according to multiple social contexts.

For instance, someone who thinks of themselves as being an extrovert may also greatly cherish his or her own company or time alone. These are not extreme extroverts.

They possess a milder degree of extrovert qualities as compared to someone who does not enjoy being alone even for a minute and constantly craves company.

Here are eight types of extrovert personalities that will give you an even more informed and precise insight about the people you are analyzing.

ESTP – Extroverted, Sensing, Thinking, Perceiving

ESTPs are outgoing people who employ a more logical and practical approach in dealing with their problems. They are focused on getting quick results and resolutions. They are very effective when it comes to reading people by picking various clues. These guys are action-oriented and prefer real actions over abstract ideas.

The ESTP approach towards problem-solving is proactive and energetic. ESTPs are focused, attentive, and spontaneous. Their best approach to learning or gaining knowledge is by taking things into action. These are the hands-on action takers and solution seekers.

ESFP – Extroverted, Sensing, Feeling, Perceiving

ESFP are primarily loving, outgoing, accommodating, flexible, friendly, and mediating by nature. They chase new experiences and possibilities and are always open to trying something unique and offbeat. The ESFPs are more positive and optimistic by nature.

They are excellent team members and love combine forces or synergizing with others to achieve fantastic outcomes. These are the people who believe in enjoying and living life to the fullest while forging strong bonds with others. Under stress and expectations, they tend to become more insecure and pessimistic.

ENFP – Extroverted, Intuitive, Feeling, Perceiving

ENFPs are warm, energetic, enthusiastic, and bright folks who possess most qualities to lead a successful and fulfilling life. They are innately creative and perceive the world as being full of varied possibilities that can do justice to their potential. ENFPs have a more varied range of passions and interests.

These people excel at doing things they are passionate about. When they are caught in more unpleasant situations or non-beneficial circumstances, they can smooth talk or manipulate others into having their way.

ENTP – Extroverted, Intuitive, Thinking, and Perceiving

These are the concept or idea folks, who instinctively read people and circumstances. They are quick decision makers (or action takers), extremely attentive or alert and straightforward. ENTPs tend to focus more on possibilities than particular plans.

These are the conversationists who leave everyone spellbound through their words. ENTPs abhor routine and look for newer/richer experiences. They are competent at analyzing people and have great respect for knowledge and varied possibilities.

ESTJ – Extroverted, Sensing, Thinking, and Judging

ESTJs appreciate and exist at the moment. They tend to display a keen sense of respect for all things traditional and established by law. There is a very clear value system that guides their actions, and they'll seldom deflect from it. ESTJ people have a fairly evolved idea of how to resolve things quickly and efficiently, thus making them suitable for leadership roles. They are practical, logical, and highly realistic by nature.

These folks excel at putting together cumbersome and complicated projects and are likely to be dependable in getting things done with painstaking attention to detail. There is a lot of hard work invested into every task they take-up, which makes them effectual project leaders. Type ESTJ places a lot of emphasis on social order, law, and security.

ESFJ – Extroverted, Sensing, Feeling, and Judging

ESFJs are people's persons. They enjoy being surrounded by people all the time and take a keen interest in getting to know others well. There is very powerful desire to be loved, accepted and be respected by others.

They want everything around them to be positive and harmonious, which makes them go out of the way to support others. ESFJs are especially skilled when it comes to making others feel wonderful about themselves. One of the reasons why they are so popular or loved or appreciated by others is because of their ability to make people around them feel special.

Their value system is more influenced by those around them. It adapts and varies according to people and situations. Being appreciated and contributing to the larger welfare of mankind is what they essentially thrive in.

ENFJ – Extroverted, Intuitive, Feeling, and Judging

ENFJ people possess excellent people skills and are known to be empathetic, compassionate, affectionate, and responsible. They are more outwardly focused, and do not enjoy their own company. They display an excellent knack for spotting potential in other people. Not just that, they also tend to go out of the way in helping people realize their true potential. ENFJ people are faithful, and accept both appreciation and criticism with ease.

ENTJ – Extroverted, Intuitive, Thinking and Judging

ENTJs are outspoken, clear in their decisions, and easily take to leadership positions. For them, the world is filled with options and possibilities. They tend to view problems as challenges. ENTJs are ambitious, career-oriented, and constantly looking for different ways to convert problems into workable and practical solutions.

These people thrive in setting long terms goals and fulfilling them. ENTJ people tend to be well informed, knowledgeable, and aggressive when it comes to presenting their ideas. Even though they aren't intuitively tuned in to the feelings of other people, they can be increasingly sentimental and emotional.

Chapter Ten:

Examples of How to Read People

Now that we pretty much know the secrets of reading people, let's look at some real-life illustrative examples of how we can read people comprehensively and accurately.

Scenario One

Let's assume you are out on a blind date. You do not know much about the person except what you have probably heard from a friend who has set you both up. How can you put together verbal and non-verbal clues to determine if they are indeed a perfect match for you?

Of course, it's not going to be easy when it comes to decoding a person's behavior through his or her body language on a date because generally, people are in their best behavior when out on a date to charm their potential partner.

Develop a keen eye for observing verbal and nonverbal clues. How guarded is someone with his or her body language? On a first date, people aren't generally very open. They will most likely cross their limbs and maintain a considerable physical distance. Similarly, their palms will be inward facing.

However, as time passes and you move on to the second or third date, you will begin to notice visible changes in the demeanor of the person. Rigid postures soon convert into more relaxed, warm, and inviting body language.

How do you feel about the other person being more comfortable and open in your presence? There is a powerful principle known as *mirroring*. This one simple technique can make you more likable and appealing to others.

Mirroring is nothing but following or mimicking a person's actions in a more subtle way. You can mimic the way a person is holding his or her glass, take a sip of the drink after he or she does, gesticulate like him or her, or even use the words he or she does. Be careful that it does not come across as if you are making fun of them or mocking them.

Mirroring works brilliantly on a subconscious level. The person is more likely to feel you are one of his or her own kind if you, at a subconscious level, mirror his or her actions. The person will instantly connect with you and feel more at ease in your company.

Similarly, when someone else is mirroring you, he or she has most likely taken a liking for you and feels relaxed in your company. If you want a more tensed looking date to relax a bit, let your own guard down and display a more relaxed body language. He or she will receive the message on a subconscious level, and their body language will soon follow suit.

Throw your arms and palms open (or uncrossed). Offer a genuine smile (yes with the crow feet, crinkles, and all) and stay in close physical proximity to the person. Avoid moving away from the date during the course of your outing. Physical distance is a huge red flag for subconsciously distancing yourself from the person.

When you notice that a person's body language changes or becomes more rigid (or closed) when you are talking about something, quickly change the topic. They are probably not very comfortable or open to discuss the subject with you yet.

Scenario Two

Now let's pick up another real-life scenario where you can apply people reading skills. You are a recruiter who is assigned the task of interviewing and selecting the best people for filling in a particular role.

This is another tricky one. If a candidate is frequently blinking, you may be likely to assume that he or she is extremely nervous. How can you be so sure that his or her lenses aren't causing discomfort? Again, avoid rushing to sweeping conclusions, and learn to identify underlying motives behind people's behavior.

Slouching is a big no-no. It can be an indicator of low self-confidence and respect for authority. The person may not be taking the interview process or job position seriously. The individual may not be an assertive and self-assured decision maker.

Similarly, I've come across plenty of people who sit on the edge of their seat. Now that's understandable when you are watching a thriller on television or the cinema, but not during job interviews. Sit in a comfortable and relaxed position.

If the candidate is sitting on the edge of the seat and leaning forward, that's a good sign. He or she is keenly tuned in to what you are speaking or wants you to hear exactly what they are saying. However, people intruding your personal space by placing themselves a little too close for comfort is again not a very positive sign.

Similarly, I also find a lot of candidates leaning behind during an interview. If you are the interviewer, this is another red flag. The person is may likely be defensive and may not accept responsibility or accountability for his or her actions.

Look at the candidate's shoulder movements carefully. If they are describing a certain experience with a lot of grandeur, but their shoulders are stiff, or there's movement in a single shoulder, he or she may not be sure of what they are saying or may be blatantly lying. Again, observe other clues before making judgments.

When a person is incessantly touching his or her face or fiddling with their hair, it can be discomforting or misleading. Similarly, continuously rubbing their neck is a sign of trying to calm themselves in a stressful situation. It can be an indication of stress due to lying too.

Crossing arms across the chest is a huge indicator of defensiveness and being close to other's ideas. These people may not be very secure and may appear distant or disconnected.

While it may be all right when someone is meeting a person for the first time or coming in contact with a stranger, the closed demeanor should slowly wear off during the course of the conversation. If it does not, the person isn't very open to your views or ideas.

While a majority of us take to fidgeting at one time or another, excessive fidgeting or playing with objects can be a huge sign of nervousness.

Some amount of anxiety and nervousness is acceptable in a job interview. However, if the person's role demands increased interaction with people and they are anxious while talking to you that is not a very healthy sign.

Strong handshakes are a sign of confidence, assertiveness, mental strength, and determination. However, too firm a handshake can also signify intimidation, control, dominance, or aggression. If a candidate is shaking your hand too firmly, it may most likely be a sign of aggressiveness, arrogance, or trying to gain the upper hand in the conversation.

This is also one area where you'll have to consider the cultural context as handshakes tend to vary from culture to culture. If handshakes are also accompanied by a genuine, warm smile, it is a good sign.

Eyes are believed to offer a glimpse into a person's soul. Direct and consistent eye contact is viewed as a sign of self-assuredness, positivity, integrity, and confidence. It is a sign for establishing trust, genuineness, and confidence. Someone who is constantly shifting their gaze and does not look into our eyes is hard to trust.

Having said that, analyzing a person's eye contact can be particularly challenging. Candidates who have a more piercing gaze can come across as intimidating, rude, and aggressive. They may even be looking down upon you.

Similarly, sometimes, not making eye contact may be a sign of nervousness and not deception. People also quickly shift their gaze when they are trying to recall or think about something.

Sometimes, counter-intuitively, people who lie may attempt to make even more eye contact to appear truthful.

Job aspirants are always under the scanner during interviews. They are aware that recruiters are closely watching and scrutinizing them. This in no way implies that body language is irrelevant or does not count.

However, a lot of the candidate's body language will depend on your own body language as a recruiter. It's not a one-way street really. A lot of people's actions and reactions are directly dependent on your behavior.

A pleasant body language on your part will allow the candidate to demonstrate a more relaxed and open demeanor. Similarly, negative body language on your part leads to greater defensiveness and reservations by the candidate.

Avoid slouching or being fidgety. These signals can subconsciously get the candidate to act in a similar manner. As a recruiter or interviewer, you need to be aware of your conscious as well as subconscious signals.

Also, a lot of times people (especially job candidates) know that their body language and verbal clues will be assessed during the course of the interview. This makes it easier for them to fake it according to what they believe will create a positive impression. However, as a trained observer of people, you'll instantly identify any behavioral inconsistencies. It's tough to fake everything at once. It is tough to fake a cluster of clues.

Sometimes, their gestures and expressions may not match their words. Other times, the tone of their voice and posture may be totally different. Trained people analyzers can spot these differences or inconsistencies.

Now there are tons of verbal clues that will give you an insight into the person's thoughts and behavior. Candidates that speak with a clear voice, while maintaining a steady volume, intonation, and rhythm are more likely to be more balanced, dependable and steady individuals who wield more rational decisions. Focus on their breath while they are speaking. Does it match the steadiness of their speech?

Talking fast or in a constantly wavering pattern can be a sign of nervousness as well as deception. If there isn't clarity of speech, you'll have to look for other signals to establish that the person is indeed lying or unsure of his abilities. You may have to watch out for other signs such as tone, gestures, posture, expressions, and words.

Filler words such as "umm," "hmmm," etc. again point to lack of conviction and self-assuredness. These guys may be slow decision makers or unsure of their abilities. People who use short, clear and simple sentence are more in control of themselves, and confident of their abilities.

Scenario 3

This is going to be fun. Imagine walking to a party or a business networking event, where you do not know anyone except the host or organizer. Everyone here is a stranger whom you have to make an attempt to get to know.

Just how will you do that? How will you determine or identify people who are open to your message and those that do not care a lark about what you are saying? Again, people reading skills to the rescue!

Let's start with my favorite, mirroring. We've discussed how mirroring is the best way to become more likable and appealing to another person. It is so effective because it's very primordial in its approach. When you lean against the wall exactly like someone whom you just met at a party or hold your glass in a manner in which they do, you are making them more comfortable in your presence.

Similarly, if a person is constantly mirroring your actions (sipping on a drink right after you or copying your expressions), he or she may have taken a liking for you at a subconscious level. They may have felt you are just like them, and hence appear more relaxed and open in your company. Next time, try mirroring people's actions when you are getting to know them, and observe the effect!

You introduce yourself and start talking to a stranger. Halfway through narrating incident or anecdote, you spot their raised eyebrows expression. What does that reveal? Well, most probably he or she is having a hard time believing what you are saying or aren't convinced about your ideas. Raised eyebrows are almost always a sign of worry, disbelief, surprise, or fear.

Just try raising your eyebrows when you are in the middle of a warm, relaxed and informal conversation with your best buddy. Is it possible? Pretty tough right? If the topic of conversation is an easy and relaxed one, it will not lead to nervousness or fear. If the topic you've initiated isn't rationally worrisome or fearful (for instance, you are telling a joke), then there's something else going on in the person's mind.

Have you ever noticed how when you are talking to or addressing a group, a couple of people in the group will be nodding excessively in an exaggerated manner? This simply means that they are highly anxious about what impression you have about them and are eager to be in your good books. These are people who are keen to make a favorable impression on you and are constantly insecure about you doubting their abilities.

Clenched jaws, furrowed brow, and tightened back and neck are indicators of huge stress. These clues reveal discomfort and lack of ease. The person may not be comfortable in your company or may be anxious about what you think about him or her. They may also be preoccupied with distress-causing thoughts. The bottom line, like always, is to find a clear incongruence between what the person is saying and what their body language is showing.

One very important thing about analyzing people through body language is paying close attention to our own involuntary reactions as observers. Be cautious how the signals you are giving out while responding to others. Reactions and responses are at times channelized by conflicting motives.

Bonus Chapter:

The Ultimate Body Language Cheat Sheet

Since I love my readers so much, I decided to throw in an ultimate body language cheat-sheet that will allow you to effectively read even the tiniest or seemingly insignificant gestures to understand the behavior, thoughts, and feelings of those around you.

Body language – Standing with hands placed on the hips
Interpretation – Aggression

--

Body language – Tapping foot or crossing legs while sitting
Interpretation – Boredom or lack of inspiration

--

Body language – Walking erect and fast
Interpretation – Sign of high confidence, self-esteem, and self-assuredness

--

Body language – Hands placed in the pockets
Interpretation – Lack of hope or dejection

--

Body language – Touching nose frequently
Interpretation – Lying, feeling rejected or doubting something

--

Body Language – Hand placed on the cheek or head
Interpretation – Thinking, contemplating, trying to come up with a solution

--

Body Language – Clasping hands behind
Interpretation – Anger, dejection, frustration and a general feeling of hopelessness

--

Body Language – Frequently rubbing the eyes
Interpretation – Disbelief, apprehension, doubt, lack of certainty

--

Body Language – Titled head or neck
Interpretation – Interest in what the speaker is saying

--

Body Language – Squeezing the nose bridge
Interpretation – Forming a negative opinion about the speaker

--

Body Language – Drumming fingers or continuously tapping away on an object.
Interpretation – Impatience, boredom, lack of inspiration

--

Body Language – Playing with hair
Interpretation – Insecurity, nervousness, lacking confidence

Body Language – Locking or twisting ankles
Interpretation – Fear, anxiety or apprehension

--

Body Language – Rubbing palms
Interpretation – Anticipation

--

Body Language – Being seated with palms clasped right behind the head
Interpretation - Reinforcing authority, power, and superiority.

--

Body Language – Open palms
Interpretation – Openness, flexibility or sincerity

--

Body Language – Frequently stroking the chin region
Interpretation - Trying to come up with a solution or make a decision

--

Body Language – Incessantly biting nails
Interpretation – Anxiety, insecurity, nervousness, worry

--

Body Language – Pulling at the ear continuously
Interpretation – Inability to come up with a solution or make a decision

--

Body Language – Head titled for long
Interpretation – Boredom or lack of inspiration

--

Body Language – Placing Finger Tips Together
Interpretation – Demonstrating authority, power or control

Body Language – Lowering head

Interpretation – Concealing something, shyness, nervousness, submissiveness, cowardice, shame, maintaining distance, disbelief or thinking deeply

--

Body Language – Sitting with legs apart

Interpretation – Open, relaxed, approachable, and comfortable, at ease with the setting or topic of conversation or company

--

Body Language – Hands closed with a pointed finger

Interpretation – Demonstration of authority or dominance

Conclusion

Thank you for getting a copy of my book *How to Analyze People: The Complete Guide to Body Language, Personality Types, Human Psychology and Speed Reading Anyone.*

I hope you enjoyed reading it and were able to learn the finer nuances of reading and analyzing people. I also hope it offered you plenty of actionable ideas, practical tips, and wisdom nuggets for boosting your people reading and analyzing skills.

Our conscious actions, involuntary subconscious actions, and reactions can rarely be controlled or manipulated. But the great news is, with consistent practice, efforts and application, it becomes easy to read people through these involuntary subconscious reactions. Improving your people analyzing skills is an evolving and dynamic process that gets better with time.

The next step is to simply go out there and use all the proven strategies mentioned in the book. You cannot suddenly become an expert at reading people. Apply the techniques mentioned in the book in your daily life, and see the results!

You'll gradually transform from a socially awkward and unaware person who struggles who understand people to a socially evolved individual, who understands people and knows how to deal with them based on how they are thinking or feeling.

Lastly, if you enjoyed reading the book, take time out to share your feedback by posting a review. It'd be highly appreciated!

Made in the USA
Lexington, KY
25 July 2018